Date: 1/29/13

J 599.789 HAU
Haugen, Brenda.
Giant pandas /

Endangered and Threatened Animals

GIANT PANDAS

by Brenda Haugen

Consultant:
Colby Loucks
Director
Conservation Science Program, World Wildlife Fund

CAPSTONE PRESS
a capstone imprint

Snap Books are published by Capstone Press,
1710 Roe Crest Drive, North Mankato, Minnesota 56003.
www.capstonepub.com

Library of Congress Cataloging-in-Publication Data
Haugen, Brenda.
  Giant pandas / by Brenda Haugen.
     p. cm. — (Snap. Endangered and threatened animals)
  Includes bibliographical references and index.
  Summary: "Describes the life cycle and characteristics of pandas, including physical and
    environmental threats to the species"—Provided by publisher.
  ISBN 978-1-4296-8663-1 (library binding)
  ISBN 978-1-62065-346-3 (ebook PDF)
  1. Giant panda—Juvenile literature. 2. Giant panda—Life cycles—Juvenile literature.
  3. Endangered species—Juvenile literature. I. Title.

  QL737.C214H38 2013
  599.789—dc23   2012000041

Editor: Mari Bolte
Designer: Bobbie Nuytten
Media Researcher: Marcie Spence
Production Specialist: Kathy McColley

Photo Credits:
Alamy: Dennis Cox, 23, Keren Su/China Span, 14, 19 (panda), Malcolm Fairman, 22, Mohammed Abidally, 19 (left);
Corbis: Reuters, 15 (top); Shutterstock: 06photo, 8, Aloxey, design element, Dani Vincek, 17, df028, 11 (top right),
Eric Isselee, 11 (bottom), 13, 15 (middle and bottom), 27, Henry Tsui, 19 (house), Hung Chung Chih, 11 (top left),
16, 19 (habitat), 20, 24, 25, 29, Khoroshunova Olga, 5, Kinetic Imagery, 28, Mackey Creations, design element,
RCPHOTO, cover, Sergio Schnitzler, 19 (right), Subbotina Anna, 9

Printed in the United States of America in North Mankato, Minnesota.
042012   006682CGF12

Table of Contents

One Rare Bear

On a cold, wet mountain in central China, a black and white bear sits in a dimly lit forest. Sunlight streams through the coniferous trees, shining its light on the bamboo growing beneath. The giant panda chews a stalk of the woody grass. Its powerful jaws make quick work of its meal. The panda is in no hurry. The shy animal will move only about 500 yards (457 meters) all day. Pandas spend most of their waking hours filling their round bellies with bamboo.

Many **species** of bamboo grow in the forests. Despite the variety, pandas only like 25 types of bamboo. And only a few are found where pandas call home. But that's not all. Fewer forests mean fewer pandas. This unique bear is disappearing.

Black and White, but Why?

Nobody knows why giant pandas are black and white. Some people think it may be for camouflage. Others believe the colors are a warning to predators or used to attract mates.

An Unusual Diet

Most bears eat a variety of foods. But giant pandas are not like other bears. Ninety-nine percent of their diet is bamboo. They eat the entire plant, including the stalks, leaves, and shoots.

But bamboo isn't very **nutritious**. An adult panda needs to eat between 26 to 83 pounds (12 to 38 kilograms) of bamboo every day. The 1 percent of a giant panda's diet that isn't bamboo includes a variety of foods. Pandas munch on fruit, vegetables, rodents, and grasses.

Pandas spend 12 to 14 hours a day finding food. Then they spend several hours resting to digest their meals.

species: a group of plants or animals that share common characteristics

nutritious: containing elements the body uses to stay strong and healthy

Giant pandas have roamed southern and eastern China
for 2 million years. They also lived in nearby Myanmar
and North Vietnam. They lived in the bamboo forests that
covered most of the land.

Logging and farming destroyed most of the giant panda's home. In the mid-1970s to 1980s, panda **habitats** were reduced to about 5,000 square miles (13,000 square kilometers). Pandas were forced to live higher and higher up the mountains.

Today pandas are limited to 20 patches of forest habitat. The patches are scattered across six mountain ranges in China. Today this once-plentiful species now has about 1,600 individual bears in the wild.

Logging in panda territory has been illegal since 1998. But the damage was done. Lower slopes and valleys that once connected the bamboo forests were stripped of trees. Roads, cities, and other developments were built in those areas. Panda territory kept getting smaller. Today pandas are listed as endangered—at risk of dying out. Without help, they could soon be **extinct**.

habitat: the natural place and conditions in which a plant or animal lives

extinct: an animal that has died out with no more of its kind

Pandas avoid areas where trees have been cut down. They live in heavily forested areas. Even if bamboo is still growing, they will avoid treeless bamboo forests. As their lower slope habitat is lost, they become **isolated** in smaller and smaller patches of bamboo. This isolation causes big problems for pandas. It makes it more challenging to find mates. It also makes it difficult to find new areas of bamboo during bamboo die-offs.

A single panda needs around 2.5 to 4 square miles (6.5 to 10.4 square kilometers) of land to survive. Roads have cut large areas into small, unusable spaces.

isolated: all alone

Bamboo Die-offs

Bamboo is a flowering plant. Depending on the species, flowering can happen every 15 to 120 years. Whole bamboo forests can die off after flowering. It can take 10 years for a bamboo forest to be able to support pandas again.

In the past, pandas would simply move to another forest to find food. Now farms, roads, and towns stand between the bamboo patches. When the paths between bamboo forests are cut off, pandas may die along with their food source.

Chapter 2

Bear Bodies and Bamboo

Many of a giant panda's features make it look like a big, furry baby. But looks can be misleading. Those chubby cheeks are actually strong muscles designed to chew bamboo. Large, fur-covered paws act like snowshoes, allowing the panda to walk on snow and ice. A furry double coat keeps the panda warm and dry in the cool mountains. A layer of short, thick fur is covered by another layer of longer, coarse hair. The hair is slightly oily, making it water-resistant.

A giant panda is made for eating bamboo. Its front paws have long thumblike wrist bones used to hold the bamboo. The panda's 42 sharp teeth cut through the woody stalks. Strong jaws and large, flat molars crush and chew. A panda's throat and stomach have strong linings to protect the bear's insides from the sharp bamboo.

6 feet
(1.8 m)

4 feet
(1.2 m)

front paws and long wrist bones
made for handling bamboo

strong jaw and flat molars
made for crushing bamboo

double layer of hair keep
the animal warm and dry

throat and stomach
have tough linings to
help digest bamboo

fur-padded paws help
the panda walk on snow and ice

The Life of a Giant Panda

Chapter 3

Pandas are fully grown around 4 or 5 years old. Mating usually takes place between March and May. Females only mate once a year. Their ability to become pregnant may only last a few hours. This creates a big problem. Isolated males have to travel long distances to reach the female. By the time a male arrives, the female may no longer be ready to mate.

When a female is ready to mate, she attracts a male by making bleating sounds and marking her territory. Sometimes more than one male will respond. The competing males may push each another around. They may even stand up on their hind legs and lunge and grab at their opponent. Usually the biggest male wins the battle and the right to mate.

What's that Noise?

Though giant pandas are usually quiet, they make many noises. They honk when upset and squeal when afraid or under threat. They huff or snort when they are nervous or are trying to threaten another animal. A male may roar at another male when they are fighting over a female during mating season. A female may roar at a male that won't leave her alone. Pandas also bleat, moan, bark, and chirp.

13

Pregnant pandas find a safe place, such as a cave or a hollow tree, to give birth. About 129 to 159 days after mating, one or two cubs are born. Panda cubs are born without hair. Their little pink bodies are about the size of a stick of butter. At birth, a panda cub weighs around 3.5 ounces (100 grams).

If twins are born, the second cub often dies. In the wild, female pandas will only care for one cub at a time. Raising a newborn cub is hard work. The mother panda won't leave her den to eat for at least two to three weeks. Pandas are unable to store fat like other bears. This period without eating tires the mother.

Panda cubs are usually born in August, September, or October.

Cub to Adult

- Birth weight: 3.5 ounces (100 grams)

- 3 weeks old: cub has black and white markings it will have in adulthood

- 75 days old: eyes open completely

- 100 days: cub weighs about 13 pounds (6 kilograms)

- 5 to 6 months old: cub begins to eat bamboo leaves

- 8 to 9 months old: cub is weaned

- 1 year old: cub weighs about 80 pounds (36 kg)

- 2 to 3 years: cub leaves its mother

- 4 to 5 years: panda will mate for the first time

A female panda will typically have fewer than seven cubs in a lifetime. This means that panda populations grow slowly. Breeding centers and zoos are helping increase the number of pandas.

The Chengdu Panda Breeding and Research Center in China has had one of the most successful breeding programs in the world. More than 160 cubs have been born and raised there since 1987. The Wolong Nature **Reserve**, also in China, has raised more than 120 cubs. Worldwide, around 300 pandas have been raised in **captivity**. Today cubs in captivity have a 94 percent survival rate. It is hoped that these cubs can someday be released into the wild. With only 1,600 pandas in the wild, scientists hope these captive-bred cubs will increase the wild population.

In 1963 scientists successfully bred the first panda in captivity. The 300th captive-bred panda was born in 2010.

Into the Wild

Since the early 1980s, 10 captive pandas have been set free. However, only two successfully **adapted** to wild life. Some died in the wild. Others were unable to gain weight and returned to the breeding centers.

In January 2012, the Chengdu Panda Breeding and Research Center released six pandas into "Panda Valley." This protected forest is part of the center. It is designed to teach pandas how to live in the wild. The pandas released were chosen from 108 pandas at the center. If the project is successful, scientists hope to release 100 pandas in the next 50 years.

reserve: an area of land set aside by the government for a special purpose, such as protecting plants and animals

captivity: the condition of being kept in a cage

adapt: to change in order to survive

Chapter 4

Endangered!

Giant pandas are one of the rarest animals on Earth. People pose the biggest threat to the panda's survival. China's population continues to grow. More land is cleared for farming, roads, and other developments. When pandas and people compete for space, food, and other resources, the humans usually win.

Poachers are always a big threat to rare animals. With their limited wild population, the loss of a few pandas is devastating. A panda fur can bring in more than $60,000. In recent years, the direct poaching of pandas has declined. But pandas are still caught and killed in traps and snares meant for other animals, such as musk deer or black bears.

In 1984 the Convention on International Trade in Endangered Species (CITES) met. They listed giant pandas as endangered. The 171 nations of CITES were expected to pass laws to protect endangered animals.

Threats to the Giant Panda

POACHING AND HUNTING

HABITAT LOSS

HUMAN DEVELOPMENT

LOW REPRODUCTIVE RATES

ILLEGAL LOGGING

poacher: a person who hunts or fishes illegally

19

To give giant pandas more room, more than 50 nature reserves were created in China. The reserves protected around 2.5 million acres (1 million hectares) to the panda's habitat.

Included in the new reserves are more than 1.2 million acres (500,000 hectares) of land in China's Minshan Mountains. This mountain range is home to nearly half of all wild pandas.

About three of every five wild pandas live in a reserve.

In addition, eight new reserves and five **corridors** were made in the Qinling Mountains. One-fifth of the wild panda population lives there. The Chinese government has created 10 corridors in the two mountain ranges. It is hoped that these corridors will link panda habitats and populations.

Reserves and Corridors

Key
- current panda range
- panda reserves

China

Gansu

Qinling Mtns.

Shaanxi

Minshan Mtns.

Qionglai Mtns.

•Chengdu

Xiangling Mtns.

Sichuan

Liangshan Mtns.

corridor: a narrow strip of land

But people also live in and around those reserves. For example, four native groups live around the Wolong Nature Reserve. Many of these people lived around the reserve long before the land was set aside for pandas. Between 1975 and 1996, the number of people living in this reserve increased by 66 percent. The people harvested bamboo for food. They cut down trees for fuel and building material. Pandas are caught in traps and snares the people set for other animals.

About one-third of the bamboo used around the world comes from China.

A study in 1996 showed that logging made up 60 percent of China's industry. It also showed that logging was quickly destroying the panda's habitat. The Chinese government has tried to stop activities that are harmful to pandas. And the people who share the land understand that pandas need help.

In 1998 logging in panda territory was banned.

Making Connections

China's Highway 108 once ran through panda habitat in the Qinling Mountains. The road split two large panda populations. To bring the pandas together, an 11-mile (18-km) tunnel was built through the mountains for drivers. The $410 million tunnel opened January 20, 1997. Then about 500 acres (200 hectares) of bamboo were planted to reconnect the panda habitats.

China has begun restoring panda territory by planting trees. Though growing trees takes time, the number of giant pandas living in the wild has already started to increase. Counts done in the 1970s and 1980s both found about 1,000 pandas. Now there are about 1,600.

Organizations such as the World Wildlife Fund have also been working with people who live in or near the reserves. Some people have been given jobs at the panda research stations. They are trained in wildlife management and conservation. They also learn how to watch the reserves' borders and keep out poachers. When their jobs are tied to the pandas' survival, people are more likely to try to save the animals.

The panda has been the mascot of the World Wildlife Fund since the organization was founded in 1961.

Researchers at panda stations around the world are learning all they can about these rare creatures.

Umbrella Species

Pandas aren't the only creatures benefiting from the reserves. Many other species, such as the takin, golden monkey, and crested ibis also live in the area. Pandas are what's known as an umbrella species. Protecting them means many other species are protected too.

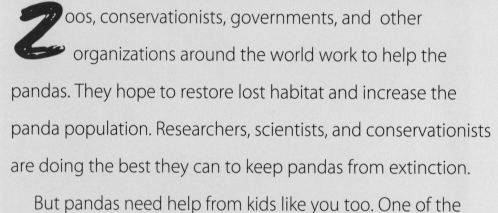

Chapter 5

Good News for a Beloved Bear

Zoos, conservationists, governments, and other organizations around the world work to help the pandas. They hope to restore lost habitat and increase the panda population. Researchers, scientists, and conservationists are doing the best they can to keep pandas from extinction.

But pandas need help from kids like you too. One of the best things you can do for pandas is to learn more about them. Visit a zoo to see pandas up close. Watch a documentary featuring pandas in the wild. Go to your local library and check out some books about these rare creatures.

Pandas in Zoos

The U.S. Fish and Wildlife Service saw that many zoos and organizations were asking for pandas. In 1998 a new law banned the import of pandas to the United States. Any zoos wanting pandas would have to agree to aid in the scientific study of pandas. They also had to participate in panda breeding programs.

More about Pandas

The Internet is full of sites about pandas. Look up the places below, and then share what you've learned with your friends and family!

- **National Geographic Kids** has tons of panda-related games, pictures, and facts. Solve a panda puzzle. Watch a video of pandas in the wild. And read about what it's like to raise panda cubs in captivity.

- **The National Zoo** has all kinds of information about pandas. Meet the zoo's pandas, Mei Xiang and Tien Tien. Check out their habitat, and read interviews from the panda keepers. Use the Pandacam to watch the pandas at play or click through photo albums of a panda cub.

- **The World Wildlife Fund** is the world's leading conservation organization. Visit their Web site to learn more about the threats pandas face and what you can do to help. Send a friend an e-card, view their panda photo album, and find out how you can adopt a panda.

Have you ever been to a Panda Party? Throwing one yourself is easy, and Pandas International can help. This group supplies a variety of fun items, such as panda bracelets, postcards, stickers, and photographs, to help raise awareness about pandas.

Organizations such as Pandas International, the World Wildlife Fund, and even your local zoo can always use help. You don't have to raise a million dollars to make a difference. Students at one middle school participated in Pennies 4 Pandas, another program sponsored by Pandas International. The students at Sky Vista Middle School in Colorado collected pennies to help their favorite bear. One sixth-grader raised 7,000 pennies alone! All together, the class was able to raise more than $1,200.

With help, the panda can begin to make a comeback.

People of all ages are working together to save their beloved bear. Their efforts are paying off. The panda population continues to grow. But the work isn't done. If you want to help, you can follow the examples of other kids who are making a difference. Or maybe you have a great idea of your own. With a little imagination and a bit of effort, you can help save the giant panda too.

Glossary

adapt (uh-DAPT)—to change in order to survive

captivity (kap-TIV-ih-tee)—the condition of being kept in a cage

coniferous (kuh-NIF-ur-uhss)—trees that produce cones and have needles instead of leaves

corridor (KOR-uh-dor)—a narrow strip of land

digest (dy-GEST)—to break down food so it can be used by the body

extinct (ik-STINGKT)—no longer living; an extinct animal is one that has died out, with no more of its kind

habitat (HAB-uh-tat)—the natural place and conditions in which an animal or plant lives

isolated (eye-suh-LAYT-ed)—all alone

molar (MOH-lur)—wide teeth used to chew food

nutritious (noo-TRISH-uhss)—containing elements the body uses to stay strong and healthy

poacher (POHCH-ur)—a person who hunts or fishes illegally

reserve (ri-ZURV)—an area of land set aside by the government for a special purpose, such as protecting plants and animals

species (SPEE-sheez)—a group of plants or animals that share common characteristics

wean (WEEN)—to stop depending on a mother's milk

Read More

Allen, Kathy. *Giant Pandas in a Shrinking Forest: A Cause and Effect Investigation*. Animals on the Edge. Mankato, Minn.: Capstone Press, 2011.

Gish, Melissa. *Pandas*. Living Wild. Mankato, Minn.: Creative Education, 2012.

Zeiger, Jennifer. *Pandas*. Nature's Children. New York: Children's Press, 2012.

Internet Sites

FactHound offers a safe, fun way to find Internet sites related to this book. All of the sites on FactHound have been researched by our staff.

Here's all you do:

Visit *www.facthound.com*

Type in this code: 9781429686631

Super-cool stuff!

Check out projects, games and lots more at
www.capstonekids.com

Index